938
Coh

Cohen, Daniel.
Ancient Greece

DATE DUE		PERMA-BOUND

938
Coh

Cohen, Daniel.
Ancient Greece

DATE DUE	BORROWER'S NAME	RM. NO.
	Luigi	

4

THE CITY OF ATHENS

1–THE ACROPOLIS,
     site of the temple dedicated to Athena

2–STOA OF ZEUS,
     dedicated to the chief Greek god

3–BOULEUTERION,
     a meeting place where the leading
     people of the city held assembly

4–TEMPLE OF HEPHAESTUS,
     dedicated to the divine craftsman

ANCIENTGREECE

By Daniel Cohen

Illustrated by James Seward

Doubleday

NEW YORK LONDON TORONTO SYDNEY AUCKLAND

The editor wishes to thank Danielle
Arnold, Department of the Classics,
Harvard University, for her careful
review of the manuscript and
illustrations.

Published by Doubleday
a division of
Bantam Doubleday Dell Publishing
Group, Inc., 666 Fifth Avenue
New York, New York 10103
Doubleday and the portrayal of an
anchor with a dolphin are trademarks of
Doubleday, a division of Bantam
Doubleday Dell Publishing Group, Inc.
Library of Congress
Cataloging-in-Publication Data
Cohen, Daniel.
    Ancient Greece / by Daniel Cohen ;
illustrated by James Seward
1st ed.
     p. cm.
    Includes index.
    Summary: Focuses on the
personalities and historical events which
shaped the civilization of ancient
Greece, from the story of the Trojan
War to the conquests of Alexander the
Great.
    ISBN 0-385-26064-4.
    ISBN 0-385-26065-2 (lib. bdg.)
    1. Greece—Civilization—To 146
B.C.—Juvenile literature. [1. Greece—
Civilization—To 146 B.C. 2. Greece—
History—To 146 B.C.]
I. Seward, James, ill. II. Title.
DF77.C68 1990   89-30735
938—dc19 CIP AC
RL: 3.7

A Hero's Anger

"**L**et me tell you of the anger of Achilles (uh-kil'-eez)." So begins the most famous story of ancient Greece. It is set during the time of the Trojan War. Ilium is another name for Troy, and the story is called the *Iliad*.

According to the *Iliad* the war began when Paris, son of the king of Troy, ran off with the beautiful Helen, wife of King Menelaus (meh'-neh-lay'-us) of Sparta (spar'-tuh). Menelaus called on his powerful brother, King Agamemnon (ag'-uh-mem'-non) of Mycenae (migh-see'-nee), to help him avenge this wrong. Agamemnon gathered an army from many other Greek cities to attack Troy.

But Troy had strong walls and was well defended, so the war dragged on for ten years. A quarrel broke out between Agamemnon and Achilles, greatest of the Greek warriors. Achilles simply quit the battle and stayed in his tent. When Achilles' best friend was slain by Hector, the Trojan champion, Achilles came roaring out of his tent and killed Hector. Without the powerful Hector at the battlefront, the doom of Troy was sealed.

There is a second Trojan epic, the *Odyssey* (odd'-es-see). It tells of the adventures of Odysseus (oh-dis'-yoos), another Greek warrior, during his ten-year attempt to get home after the end of the Trojan War.

The Blind Poet

The *Iliad* and the *Odyssey* were said to have been composed by a blind poet named Homer who lived around 750 B.C. They were meant to be recited at banquets or other gatherings.

The *Iliad* and the *Odyssey* were also written down and after Homer's death they continued to be recited and read throughout the Greek world for hundreds of years. They have been called "the Bible of Greece." Even today, some 2,700 years after they were first written, they are still considered among the greatest works of literature.

But are they true? Some scholars are not even sure whether Homer existed. They think the *Iliad* and *Odyssey* are the work of many different poets. Certainly there must have been different versions of the events of the Trojan War. The war took place hundreds of years before Homer lived. Lots of incidents in the stories, like the way the gods would directly interfere in the lives of men, were clearly imaginary. No one even knew where Troy was.

A hundred and fifty years ago most scholars thought the whole story of the Trojan War was a myth. A young German boy named Heinrich Schliemann read the *Iliad* and the *Odyssey* and was convinced the basic story was real history. He made his goal in life finding the ruins of ancient Troy.

Schliemann was born poor, but he had enormous talent and energy. He became a millionaire and in 1864 he quit business and devoted his life and fortune to his search. From the descriptions in the *Iliad* he became convinced that Troy was located in the northwest corner of what is now Turkey.

Schliemann began digging and found ruins of not one city but a series of them, built one on top of the other. Today almost everyone agrees that one of those cities was Homer's Troy.

Golden Mycenae

Agamemnon, leader of the Greeks, came from Mycenae, a rich and powerful city. Homer often referred to the city as "rich in gold." This was where Heinrich Schliemann next directed his restless energy.

There was never any doubt about the location of Mycenae. There were ancient ruins on the site, but no one paid much attention to them until Schliemann began digging in 1876. Very quickly he uncovered rich graves. "The bodies were literally covered with gold and jewels," he wrote.

At the time, Schliemann was sure he had found the graves of Agamemnon and other heroes of Homer's tales. But we now know the graves were hundreds of years older. What is important is that Schliemann had begun to uncover what he called "an entirely new and unsuspected world."

Between about 1400 B.C. and 1100 B.C. Greece was dominated by powerful and wealthy cities ruled by kings who were seafarers, merchants and warriors. We now call this period the Mycenaean Age (migh-see-nee'-an).

Later Greeks looked back to the Mycenaean Age as a time of great heroes and mighty deeds. Homer's epics are set late in the Mycenaean Age. The mighty Hercules (her'-ku-leez) was said to have lived in that era. But there was a time of greatness even before the Mycenaean Age, and once again a legend provided the clue.

The Bull of Minos

Crete is a large island located to the south of Greece. According to legend, in ancient times it was ruled by a powerful king named Minos (migh'-nos). The king kept a monster that was half man, half bull, called the Minotaur (mi'-noh-tor'), in a building that was a mass of rooms and corridors so confusing that once you got in, you could never get out. It was called the labyrinth (lab'-er-inth).

Schliemann was interested in Crete, but he died before he did much digging there. The real work of discovery was made by the Englishman Arthur Evans. Evans began digging at the ancient city of Knossos (knoss'-us) on Crete in 1900. Over the next twenty-five years he brought to light a rich and luxurious civilization we now call Minoan (mi-noh'-an).

At Knossos, Evans found the remains of a huge building that was a confusing mass of rooms and corridors—a labyrinth. Everywhere there were images of bulls. These discoveries seemed to confirm the ancient legend.

The Minoans were great merchants and sailors. They were very influential in Greece for hundreds of years. Then around 1400 B.C. Minoan civilization began to crumble. According to the legend, the monster Minotaur was killed by the Greek hero Theseus (thee'-see-us). This may have been a symbol of Greek rebellion against Minoan domination. Natural disasters may also have weakened the Minoans. There is evidence that Knossos was shaken by natural disasters.

And there is another possibility. That story too is in a popular legend.

The Sinking of Atlantis

The Greek philosopher Plato (play'-toe) told the story of Atlantis, a great continent in the middle of the Atlantic Ocean. He said that the people of Atlantis became so proud they angered the gods. So the gods destroyed Atlantis by causing it to sink into the sea. Ever since Plato first wrote the story of Atlantis, people have been trying to locate the "lost continent." Today, scientists are sure that such a continent could not have existed.

Most scholars and scientists assumed that Atlantis was a myth. But over the last thirty years a new theory has been developed. Scientists have found evidence that around 1400 B.C. there was a gigantic volcanic explosion, not in the Atlantic, but in the Aegean Sea, just south of Greece. The explosion was on the volcanic island of Thera, near Crete. It caused a large portion of the island to sink into the sea.

At the time Thera contained a Minoan city which was destroyed in the disaster. Tidal waves from the explosion could have swamped the harbors of Crete and Greece. Ash from the explosion could have fallen on the fields and ruined the crops. A disaster of this size could have weakened Minoan civilization, which went into severe decline about that time. Over a thousand years later, memories of the sinking of Thera and the destruction of Minoan civilization may have been reflected in the legend of Atlantis.

We cannot be sure about Atlantis, or about Homer's Troy or the Minotaur, or many of the other ancient Greek myths and legends. They are not history. And they can be interpreted in many different ways. But we should soon know more about the sunken island of Thera. Scientists are still digging there and will continue for many years.

Who Were the Greeks?

The modern nation of Greece is a small country at the southeastern edge of Europe, jutting into the Mediterranean Sea. But in ancient times there was no Greek nation. And the Greeks didn't live just in Greece, they lived all around the Mediterranean in what is now Italy and Spain, and parts of the Middle East, Asia and North Africa.

What made them Greeks was that they all spoke a common language. There were different forms of the language, or dialects—but the Greeks could usually understand one another. They called themselves Hellenes. They called everyone else—that is, everyone who did not speak Greek—barbarians. Originally that meant "people who speak funny." Later "barbarian" came to mean "uncivilized" and "savage." The ancient Greeks thought very highly of themselves.

Greece is a harsh and dry land, broken up by many mountains. The people lived in tribes, small kingdoms, and later in independent cities called a city-state or polis (poh'-lis). They were often at war with one another, and were never able to get together to form a single nation, like ancient Egypt or ancient Rome. Besides, the Greeks didn't want to get together— independence was what they prized most highly.

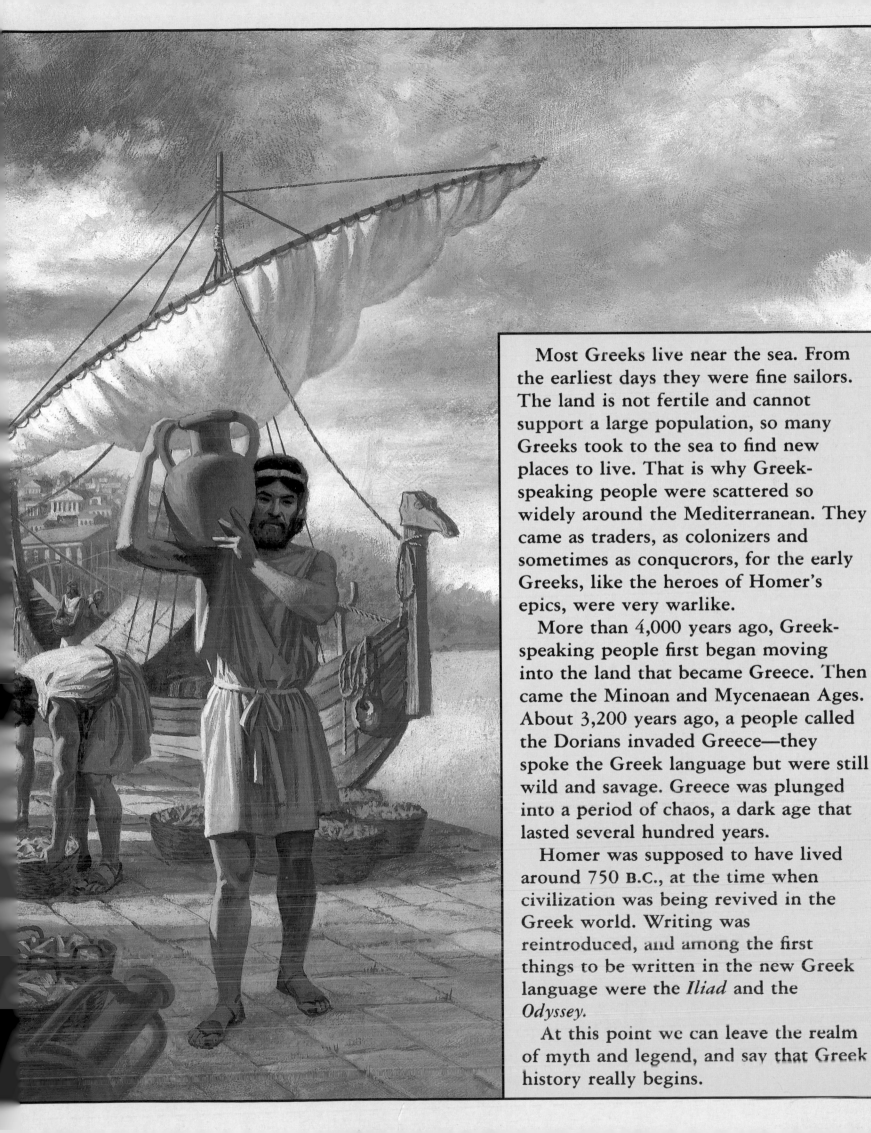

Most Greeks live near the sea. From the earliest days they were fine sailors. The land is not fertile and cannot support a large population, so many Greeks took to the sea to find new places to live. That is why Greek-speaking people were scattered so widely around the Mediterranean. They came as traders, as colonizers and sometimes as conquerors, for the early Greeks, like the heroes of Homer's epics, were very warlike.

More than 4,000 years ago, Greek-speaking people first began moving into the land that became Greece. Then came the Minoan and Mycenaean Ages. About 3,200 years ago, a people called the Dorians invaded Greece—they spoke the Greek language but were still wild and savage. Greece was plunged into a period of chaos, a dark age that lasted several hundred years.

Homer was supposed to have lived around 750 B.C., at the time when civilization was being revived in the Greek world. Writing was reintroduced, and among the first things to be written in the new Greek language were the *Iliad* and the *Odyssey*.

At this point we can leave the realm of myth and legend, and say that Greek history really begins.

The Olympics

The Greeks loved athletics. Every city, every town held regular athletic contests or games. The most famous games in Greece, the most famous games in the whole world, were held at a place called Olympia and the games were called the Olympics. Both the place and the games were named in honor of Zeus, chief god of the Greeks, who was said to dwell on Mount Olympus. The event was held once every four years.

Games of some sort were being held at Olympia long before anyone could keep written records. The first games that can be dated with any degree of accuracy were held in 776 B.C. That is also the first date in Greek history regarded as historical rather than legendary.

The earliest games were simple, just one short race. Later longer races and other events like javelin and discus throwing, boxing, wrestling and chariot racing were added.

There were no team sports; everyone competed as an individual. The games drew athletes from all parts of Greece and as many as 50,000 spectators for the five-day event. The games were considered so important that the quarrelsome Greeks even suspended their wars during the period of the games.

Athletes competed for glory, not for gold. Winners were given only a wreath of leaves woven from the sacred olive tree. But they became heroes in their home cities. Statues were put up. Poems were written in their honor. An especially enthusiastic city might cancel a winning athlete's taxes for the rest of his life.

The Olympic games were held every four years for a period of about a thousand years. They were revived again in modern times and the first modern Olympics were held in Greece in 1896. Since then the games have been held all over the world. The hope is that the modern games will bring the people of the world closer together in peace, at least for a short time, as they once brought the people of ancient Greece together.

The Oracle at Delphi

Like Mount Olympus, Delphi (dell'-figh) was sacred to all Greeks. There, on the slopes of Mount Parnassus (pahr-nas'-us), was a temple of the god Apollo. A priestess of the god would go into a trance and inspired by Apollo answer questions about the future. She was an "oracle." There were many oracles in Greece, but the one at Delphi was far and away the most celebrated.

The Greeks took the oracle very seriously. Before going off to war or starting any other important venture, Greek leaders would consult the oracle.

The priestess' words made no sense, they had to be interpreted by priests at the shrine. There were rumors that the oracle's answers were not always honest. One city was said to have bribed the priests to give their enemy nothing but discouraging responses.

Often the oracle's messages were so vague that the questioner could make of them what he wished. Croesus (kree'-sus), king of Lydia, was one of many non-Greeks to consult the oracle and he lavished rich presents on the shrine. Croesus asked if he should attack the Persian Empire, which he very much wanted to do. The oracle told him that if he attacked he would "destroy a mighty empire." Croesus attacked, and an empire was destroyed: his own.

Later, priests at Delphi insisted that Croesus should have asked which empire.

A Military Life

The best soldiers in Greece came from Sparta. The Spartan citizens ruled over a huge number of oppressed people called helots. Outnumbered nearly ten to one, the Spartans always feared a helot revolt. Early in its history Sparta also faced a series of brutal wars with neighboring cities. As a result, all of Sparta's energy was directed toward defending itself.

The life of the Spartan was not easy. At age seven or eight, a Spartan boy was taken from his family and put in a military camp. He basically remained in the army for life. A Spartan usually married when he was about twenty, but he saw his wife only briefly until their first child was born. Even then a Spartan man spent most of his time with his army unit. At age thirty, men were admitted to the Assembly, the group that ruled the state.

There were no luxuries in a Spartan's life. They did little but train and fight. Porridge was the typical meal and they slept on boards on the bare ground. The Spartan soldiers were fearless. They followed orders without question, and would die rather than retreat.

While this grim system produced fine fighting men, it squeezed almost everything else out of Spartan life. Sparta produced no famous artists, or poets, or architects, or thinkers. Even today the word "Spartan" means someone who is brave, but it also means "barren."

Spartan women, however, had much more freedom than the women of other Greek cities. Since the men were always at war or preparing for war, women had to manage households and farms. They were encouraged to take up athletic training. In addition, they dressed as they pleased.

Rule by the People

Athens (ath'-enz) was the greatest of the ancient Greek cities. One reason is that it is the place where democracy—rule by the people—was first developed.

Like most other Greek cities, Athens was once ruled by a king. Later, power was held by certain families—an aristocracy. At other times control was in the hands of a group of wealthy men —an oligarchy. Sometimes a powerful man, or tyrant, would seize power.

At the end of the sixth century B.C. Athens was a prosperous city, but a troubled one. It was on the verge of revolution.

About 594 B.C. a man named Solon (soh'-lon) was appointed archon (arh'-kon), or ruler, to try and head off the crisis. Solon acted with great boldness. He abolished many debts, and ended the practice of making slaves out of citizens who could not pay their debts. He made it illegal for a murdered man's family to take revenge on the killer. It was up to the government to punish the crime.

Solon had enormous power, but he did not choose to make himself absolute ruler, as leaders in other cities had. Instead, he strengthened the power of the Assembly—a gathering of all the citizens of Athens—which was to have the final voice in ruling the city. Sparta also had an Assembly, but the Spartans didn't take much of an interest in politics. The Athenians were always arguing and debating. They loved politics.

Solon's Athens was not a democracy as we know it today, and never became one. Slaves had no power; neither did people living in Athens who had been born in other cities, nor people who didn't own land. Women were actually worse off in democratic Athens than in militaristic Sparta. But the first steps toward democracy were taken by the Athenians, and we have every reason to be grateful to them.

There was another way in which Solon and most Athenians differed from the grim Spartans. Solon was a poet and orator. He appreciated beauty and comfort. He encouraged artists and thinkers to come to Athens, and to make it the loveliest and liveliest city on earth.

But great dangers lay ahead for Athens, and all of Greece.

The Persian Wars

The power of the Greek city-states was growing. To the east the Persian (per'-shan) Empire was also expanding. The Persians struck first at the area called Ionia (igh-oh'-nee-uh). These were Greek cities on the shore of Asia Minor. In about 499 B.C. the Ionians revolted against the Persians, and with the help of Athens and other cities, had some success. But the Persians struck back quickly, easily crushing the Ionians. Darius (duh-righ'-us), the Persian king, was determined to punish everyone who opposed him. His army prepared to attack Greece itself, particularly Athens.

As usual, the Greek city-states could not agree on what to do. Some were ready to give in to the Persians. Sparta would submit to no one, but moved very slowly. When the Persians landed on the coastal plain of Marathon (mar'-uh-thon), the Athenians had to face them almost alone.

The situation seemed hopeless, for the Greeks were greatly outnumbered. The Greek general Miltiades (mil-tigh'-uh-deez) had a bold plan. On September 12, 490 B.C., he sent his heavily armed troops charging into the Persians at a dead run. The Persians had not expected such a furious attack, and were panic-stricken and driven back to their ships. When the day was over, there were 192 Athenians dead. The Persians lost over 6,000.

It was said that Miltiades then sent the famous runner Phidippides (figh-dip'-ih-deez) to Athens, some 26 miles away, with news of the victory. He ran at top speed, without stopping, and when he reached the city, he gasped out, "We have been victorious," and died. Today the 26-mile marathon race is run in honor of Phidippides' feat.

The victory was such a stunning one that the Athenians were sure they were specially favored by the gods. In reality they had only defeated a small part of the Persian army. The Persians were not ready to give up.

Defeat and Victory

Darius was furious at the news from Marathon. He planned another and much larger attack on Greece, but died before he was able to carry out his plan. His son and successor Xerxes (zurk'-seez) had to deal with problems closer to home. It wasn't until 480 B.C., a full ten years after Marathon, that the Persians again invaded Greece.

Xerxes himself led a huge army and attacked Greece from the north. The Persian troops seemed unstoppable until in July they met a small Greek army at the narrow pass of Thermopylae (ther-mop'-ih-lee). Here a group of 300 Spartans and a few hundred of their allies held off the Persians for days. At the end they were completely surrounded, but never surrendered, and died to the last man.

The battle at Thermopylae slowed the Persians and inspired the Greeks. But it was still a Greek defeat and the Persians poured southward toward Athens. Xerxes actually entered Athens and found the city deserted. The Athenians had boarded ships for nearby islands. The Athenian fleet now confronted the Persian fleet near the island of Salamis (sal'-a-miss). The Persians had more ships, but the Greeks had better ships and better sailors. Xerxes watched in horror from a throne on the shore as the wreckage of his ships and the bodies of the crews washed up on the beach.

The defeat at Salamis took the fight out of the Persian king. He went home, but left a large force behind. The Greeks, particularly the Spartans remembering Thermopylae, fought as never before. Within a year the Persians were driven out of Greece.

How Do We Know?

We know more about the war between Greece and Persia than any war that came before it. We know about the wars of the ancient Egyptians and other early civilizations mainly from royal inscriptions. These praise the courage of the "ever victorious king"—whoever he happened to be. We have to guess as to what really took place.

When Homer wrote about the Trojan War, he was writing about something that had happened hundreds of years before he was born. In his epics the gods are always interfering. Homer wanted to tell a thrilling story.

The Persian Wars were described by Herodotus (hi-rod'-uh-tus), who was born in Ionia just about the time the wars ended. He did not witness the events he wrote about, but was able to talk to people who had. He traveled widely and learned a lot about the Greeks, Persians and other peoples. Much of this information found its way into what he wrote.

Herodotus put down what people told him, and he admitted that sometimes what he was told probably wasn't true. He just couldn't resist a good story. His main aim, however, was "to preserve a memory of the past." This he did better than anyone before him. He is therefore called "the father of history."

Greeks and Gods

In the *Odyssey* Homer wrote a scene in which Odysseus visits the underworld, called Hades, a place where the spirits of the dead go. He meets the ghost of the hero Achilles. Achilles says, "I would rather be a slave in a poor man's house than king of all the dead."

As you can see, the religion of the Olympian gods offered little comfort or joy to the average Greek. Most Greeks performed the rituals and sacrifices required, but were not deeply attached to the gods. Other religions attracted huge followings.

The town of Eleusis (ee-lyoo'-sis) near Athens was the center for one of many "mystery religions," popular in Greece. The religions were called "mystery" because the rites were supposed to be kept secret. Anyone revealing details of the ceremonies would be killed. Though thousands attended the "Eleusinian Mysteries" every year, and they were celebrated for over a thousand years, we really don't know exactly what went on.

The Eleusinian Mysteries were open to everyone who could speak Greek, women and slaves included. They gave worshipers a promise of a better life after death.

Some of the religions or cults that surrounded the god Dionysus (digh'-oh-nigh'-sus) appealed particularly to women, or were open only to women, while most other freedoms extended only to men. Women were supposed to stay at home and be quiet. Many found an outlet in the worship of Dionysus.

The ceremonies of the Olympian religion were formal and stressed self-control. The Dionysian religion was just the opposite; it featured emotional, often wild rites. One story tells of how an early Greek king scorned Dionysus and was then torn to bits by the maenads (mee'-nads), the frenzied women followers of the god.

Tragedy and Comedy

Theater in Greece grew out of religious ceremonies for Dionysus that featured group singing and dancing. Gradually different types of plays evolved. Tragedies dealt with subjects like the aftermath of the Trojan War. Comedies often made wicked fun of living people with whom everyone in the audience was familiar.

The Greeks loved theater. During major theater festivals all business in the city would be suspended. Prisoners were released. Women, barred from most public events, were allowed to attend the theater performances. Plays would begin early in the morning and citizens would eagerly sit through as many as five plays in a single day. Even in the middle of a war, with enemy troops camped right outside the walls, the people of Athens flocked to the theater.

The titles of hundreds of plays are known. Only 45 have survived completely. Even from this small number it is clear that drama was among the greatest achievements of ancient Greece.

Plays were put on in huge outdoor auditoriums. Actors wore masks so that the audience could see quickly if the character was young or old, man or woman, happy or sad. The masks had funnel-shaped mouths, which made the actor's voice sound louder so he could be heard at the back of the auditorium. The actors also wore built-up boots and heavy robes to make them look larger than life.

Lovers of Wisdom

Even deeper than the Greek love of drama was the love of knowledge. Greek thinkers called themselves "philosophers." The word means "lovers of wisdom." The Greeks asked questions about everything. They wanted to find the truth, no matter where it was. They thought about things no one had ever thought about before.

Thales (thay'-leez) has been called the first scientist. He rejected the notion that gods and demons control the universe. He said nature operated by unchanging laws, and that these laws could be discovered by observation and thought. This is the basis of all science.

Hippocrates (hih-pok'-ruh-teez) did not look to curses as the cause of disease. He did not prescribe magic as a treatment. He tried to find causes and cures in nature. Hippocrates is called the "father of medicine."

Democritus (dee-mok'-rih-tus) said that all matter was made up of tiny particles called "atoms." Anaxagoras (an'-ak-sag'-oh-ras) said the sun was an enormous flaming rock, not a god. Heraclitus (her'-uh-kligh'-tus) figured out the earth rotated on its axis and Aristarchus (ar'-i-star'-kus) said the earth and the other planets revolved around the sun. From their observations and calculations most Greek philosophers assumed the world was round.

All of these ideas, and many more, were lost or forgotten after Greek civilization declined. It took the world thousands of years to rediscover what these early Greeks already knew.

The Golden Age

At the end of the war with the Persians, Athens became the most important city in Greece. For about forty years the city had an energy and vitality unmatched in the history of the world. It has been called the Golden Age. Much of this time Athens was led by Pericles (pehr'-ih-kleez). "Future ages will wonder at us, as the present age wonders at us now," Pericles told his fellow Athenians. He was right.

Athens expanded and perfected its democracy. Every adult male citizen was not only allowed to participate in government, he was expected to. "We do not say that a man who takes no interest in politics is a man who minds his own business; we say that his business is useless," said Pericles. Athens was a large city for ancient Greece, but not large by modern standards. At its height it had only about 43,000 adult male citizens.

Athens became very rich, mainly through trade. A lot of the wealth was poured back into the city to make it beautiful. Among the many buildings constructed during this period was a temple to the goddess Athena, called the Parthenon (pahr'-the-non). The ruins of the temple still inspire visitors today. When it was first built, it contained a gigantic statue of Athena. The goddess' robe was gold; her skin was made from ivory.

The citizens of Athens believed they had the greatest city the world had ever known, and it was their mission to lead and ultimately dominate the rest of Greece. Most of the smaller cities around the Aegean Sea were absorbed in what came to be known as the Athenian Empire. The Athenian fleet ruled the sea. As the power and influence of Athens spread, it inevitably came into conflict with that other powerful Greek city-state, Sparta.

Greek vs. Greek

The war between Athens and Sparta is called the Peloponnesian War (pel'-oh-puh-nee'-shun), after the southern part of Greece where Sparta is located. The basic cause of the war was Sparta's well-founded fear that Athens was trying to dominate all of Greece. The conflict dragged on for nearly thirty years, broken by one period of peace.

Sparta still had the best army in Greece. Athens had the best navy. The Athenian plan was simple. Let Sparta attack. The Athenians pulled back behind their high city walls. The fleet kept them supplied, while the Spartans wore themselves out.

It seemed like a good plan, but in 430 B.C. something happened that no one had foreseen. A violent plague struck the crowded city. Some twenty percent of the population died, and Athens was thrown into confusion and despair. Pericles himself died, perhaps a victim of the plague.

After the death of Pericles the disheartened city was bitterly divided between those who wanted to pursue the war and those who wanted to make peace. There were more battles, more deaths on both sides. Finally in 421 B.C., ten years after the war began, a peace was agreed to. The situation was to return to just about what it had been before the war. Nothing had been accomplished; nothing had been settled. The peace was supposed to last fifty years. It lasted less than six.

Hero and Traitor

There was one man who could have been a great Athenian hero—Alcibiades (al'-sih-bigh'-uh-deez). Instead he was a disaster for the city. Alcibiades came from a powerful family and was a relative of Pericles. Rich, intelligent and charming, Alcibiades was a natural leader. He wanted to make a glorious name for himself.

The island of Sicily (off the coast of Italy) was dotted with Greek cities. The richest and most powerful was Syracuse (sir'-uh-kyoos). Alcibiades thought Athens could gain a great advantage by conquering Syracuse. In 415 B.C. he persuaded Athenian citizens to pay for an attack on Syracuse. He was to be the leader.

Once the expedition was launched, however, Alcibiades' enemies charged that he had mutilated some religious statues. The charge was probably false, but the Athenian government was angry and Alcibiades was called back. Fearing punishment, he did not return to Athens but deserted to Sparta.

The Sicilian expedition was left in the hands of Nicias (nis'-ee-us), who had opposed it in the first place. In Sparta, Alcibiades urged the Spartans to aid Syracuse. The result was a crushing defeat for Athens. However, the Spartans didn't trust Alcibiades, and in 412 B.C. he fled to Persian territory.

Athenian politics was in chaos. One faction replaced another with bewildering speed. By 410 B.C. Alcibiades was invited back to Athens. As head of the fleet, he won a number of important victories. But the Athenians could never really trust him, and in a few years he went into exile in distant Thrace.

One day Alcibiades looked down to the shore and saw the Athenian fleet anchored in what he knew was a dangerous place. He rode down to warn them, but was told Athenians needed no advice from traitors. He shrugged and rode away. A few days later the Spartan fleet suddenly appeared and destroyed the ships of Athens. It was the final blow of the long war. Weary and broke, Athens surrendered.

What of Alcibiades? He knew the Spartans were after him and fled once again to Persian territory, where he was murdered, probably by Persian orders. He had changed sides too often.

Too Many Questions

One of the most familiar figures on the streets of Athens, both before and after the war, was the philosopher Socrates (sok'-ruh-teez). He was a heavily built, homely fellow whom the Oracle at Delphi reportedly called the wisest of men. Socrates claimed he knew nothing but only asked questions. That was his method. He questioned everything, from the gods to the government.

He had many followers among the young men of Athens. He also made many powerful enemies, because he asked too many questions. After the war, Socrates was accused of corrupting the minds of the youth of Athens. Among Socrates' followers had been men like Alcibiades, who was blamed for Athens' defeat. Socrates was brought to trial, convicted and condemned to death by drinking a poison made from hemlock. He could easily have escaped but refused to do so, insisting that it was the duty of a citizen to obey the laws. He died calmly and bravely. Today, the trial and death of Socrates is one of the great stains on the history of Athens.

Socrates' most celebrated pupil was Plato. He taught that the truth about all things could be arrived at by pure thought. Plato established a school called the Academy, near Athens.

Plato's best-known student was Aristotle (ar'-ih-stot'-ul), who had a completely different point of view. Aristotle believed that wisdom could only be reached by the collection of facts. He made huge collections of everything, from plants and animals, to poetry and plays. He gathered information on government and customs. From these he tried to work out general laws of nature, politics and art.

The works of Plato and Aristotle (Socrates never wrote anything) have been read for centuries. The influence of these philosophers on the thinking of the world has been enormous. It's hard to imagine what our own civilization would be like without Socrates, Plato and Aristotle.

The Sword

Most histories of ancient Greece concentrate on Athens and Sparta. Yet there were many other cities that were important.

After the destruction of the Athenian Sicilian expedition, Syracuse rose to become the wealthiest and most powerful city in the Greek world. The city's most effective leader was Dionysius (digh'-oh-nis'-ee-us). He ruled with an iron hand from about 405 to 367 B.C.

Lots of stories were told about him. A famous one concerns a court official named Damocles (dam'-oh-kleez), who openly envied the leader's power.

Dionysius asked him if he would like to be leader for one night. Damocles jumped at the chance, and at a grand banquet he took the seat of honor. Then he looked up and saw that there was a sword pointed downward, hanging just above him. It was attached to the ceiling by a single hair. It could fall and kill him at any moment.

Dionysius explained his life was always in danger, and anyone who wanted to be leader, even for a night, had to endure a similar threat. Today we sometimes call a danger that constantly threatens a "sword of Damocles."

The Ten Thousand

At the end of the Peloponnesian War there were a lot of unemployed soldiers in Greece. A Persian prince named Cyrus (sigh'-rus) hired about ten thousand of them to help him overthrow his older brother, who had just become king. The Greeks marched right into the center of the Persian Empire and easily defeated a much larger Persian force. But during the battle Cyrus was killed. The Greeks no longer had a paymaster. So they turned around and marched back over a thousand miles to the sea, successfully fighting off the Persians all the way.

In the ancient world there were always battles and invasions. The use of hired or mercenary troops was common. The march of the ten thousand would have been a forgotten incident in history but for two reasons.

First, one of the Greeks' leaders was an educated young Athenian named Xenophon (zen'-oh-fon). He wrote an exciting and eyewitness account of the adventure called *Into the Interior.*

Second, the ease with which the ten thousand marched in and out of the once mighty Persian Empire exposed its weakness. Soon others would try to exploit that weakness with more success.

Philip of Macedonia

To the north of Greece is a land called Macedonia (mas-uh-doh'-nee-uh). The people spoke a Greek dialect. Its rulers were influenced by Greek culture. Most Greeks, however, thought of the Macedonians as little better than barbarians.

In 359 B.C. the king of Macedonia was killed. His son and heir was only a child, so the boy's tough and ambitious uncle, Philip, was made guardian. Within a few years Philip declared himself king of Macedonia.

At first the Greeks barely noticed. But Philip was not just another king of a bunch of semiwild tribesmen. Very quickly he reorganized the Macedonian army, making it one of the finest fighting forces in the world. He put down all his nearby enemies.

Philip was also a cunning politician. He played the always warring Greek city-states against one another with bribes, threats and sometimes military force. He extended his influence through Greece.

In Athens the great orator Demosthenes (dee-mos'-thih-neez) warned the people against the Macedonian king in a series of passionate speeches. But he could not rouse the Athenians. Some even began to look at Philip as the man who could unite all the Greeks in a new war against Persia.

In 337 B.C. Philip decided to divorce his wife Olympias (oh-lim'-pee-as) and remarry. There was a rumor that he also intended to make the child of his new wife the heir to his throne, rather than his son by Olympias. The next year Philip was stabbed to death while attending a religious ceremony. Many believed that the assassination had been arranged by Olympias, with the help of her young son.

The new king of Macedonia was only twenty. Demosthenes dismissed him as "a mere boy." But if the Greeks thought Macedonian power would fade, they were wrong. The young king's name was Alexander. He was to be known to the world as Alexander the Great.

Alexander the Great

Alexander's life has been the subject of many myths and legends. The reality is more amazing than the myths. He was born in 356 B.C. One of his early teachers was Aristotle.

When Alexander came to the throne, he immediately had everyone who could threaten his position put to death. He treated Greece with a mixture of savagery and respect. When the city of Thebes (theebz) revolted against Macedonian control, he had it destroyed. Yet he never touched Athens, which he regarded as the center of Greek civilization, and did not bother the fiercely anti-Macedonian Demosthenes.

At the age of twenty-two the young king led a Macedonian and Greek army to do something Greeks had dreamed of since the Persian Wars—destroy the Persian Empire. The Empire was weakened, as the march of the ten thousand had shown. Still Alexander had to fight many hard battles against much larger forces, while he was far from home. But he never lost. By 330 B.C. the defeated Persian king Darius III, fleeing from Alexander, was murdered by his own panicky bodyguards. Alexander of Macedonia became master of the vast Persian Empire.

Alexander began to believe that he was more than a king; that he was favored by the gods, or was a god himself. Persian kings had always claimed to be divine. Greek and Macedonian kings never made such claims. More and more Alexander began acting like a Persian king. He even married a Persian princess.

The Macedonian and Greek soldiers who had been Alexander's friends as well as his followers became restless with demands that they now bow before him. Besides, they had marched thousands of miles and been fighting almost constantly for years. They had collected wealth beyond their wildest dreams and were satisfied. Now they wanted to go home. But that is not what Alexander wanted.

The End of the Earth

Alexander led his increasingly unhappy troops into India, well beyond the borders of the old Persian Empire. In India he fought and won some of his most difficult battles. He planned to march across India, to what most geographers of the day thought was the ocean at the end of the world. Finally his exhausted troops would go no farther. After sulking in his tent for three days, Alexander agreed to go back. It is said he cried because he had "no more worlds to conquer."

The return was not easy. There were deserts to cross and hostile tribes to be subdued. Alexander constantly risked his own life in battle. In June, 323 B.C., Alexander the Great suddenly and mysteriously fell ill. In a few days he was dead. He was only thirty-three years old. In the brief span of ten years he had conquered the largest empire the world had ever known.

Alexander's empire did not survive his death. According to legend, just before he died, Alexander was asked who should be his successor. His answer was "the strongest." Some of his powerful generals divided up the empire among themselves, and then fought with one another for a larger share.

The real greatness of Alexander was not that he was able to establish a short-lived empire, but that he had spread Greek art and Greek ideas far beyond the Greek world. These things would survive after his death. The period following the death of Alexander is known as the Hellenistic Age.

Alexandria, a city the conqueror built in Egypt, became a world center for scientists and philosophers. Greek-style cities and towns sprang up in Syria. And in ancient India there were statues of Buddha modeled on the Greek god Apollo.

Greece and Rome

Macedonia continued to control the mainland of Greece for over a century after the death of Alexander. The Greek city-states had ceased to be major military or political powers. Increasingly, the Greek cities and Macedonia fell under the influence or direct control of a new power in the Mediterranean region—Rome.

In 214 B.C. a Roman fleet attacked Syracuse. The city held them off for nearly three years. Much of their success was attributed to Archimedes (ahr′-kih-mee′-deez), the greatest of the Greek scientists. It was said he invented special catapults and other devices that terrified the Romans. In the end, Greek brains could not withstand Roman brawn, and Syracuse fell.

It wasn't until 27 B.C. that Greece was officially made part of the Roman Empire—but the cities had lost all their independence long before that.

While Rome conquered Greece, in a way Greece also conquered Rome. The Romans read Homer and tried to claim they were descendants of the ancient Trojans. They adopted many of the Greek gods. Roman artists copied Greek statues. Roman playwrights used plots from Greek plays. Practically everything in Rome was in one way or another influenced by the Greeks.

Other civilizations had more military power and lasted longer than Greece. But none has had more impact.

The ancient Greeks really changed the history of a large part of the world. Their imagination, their spirit, their sense of what human beings could accomplish are part of what is best in our world today.

Index

About the Author

Daniel Cohen is a well-known author of more than one hundred books—many of them on science, history and the mysteries of the unknown. Several of his works have been cited as outstanding books for children by various organizations, including the Children's Book Council/ National Science Teachers Association joint committee, and the New York Public Library. He is also the author of other titles in Doubleday's line of nonfiction for young readers—*Dinosaurs, Prehistoric Animals* and *Ancient Egypt.*

Mr. Cohen resides in Port Jervis, New York, with his wife, Susan, who is also an author.

About the Artist

James Seward received a set of oil paints from his grandfather at the age of six, and has continued to paint ever since. A graduate of the Art Institute of Chicago, he began his career as an apprentice at two of Chicago's commercial art studios. He embarked on a freelance career in 1961, and since that time his paintings have appeared in many books, national ads, and calendars. He has also been commissioned to do a number of portraits, including one of Will Rogers for the Will Rogers Museum in Oklahoma.

Mr. Seward currently resides in Cleveland, Ohio, with his wife, who is also a professional artist.